Book Cover designed by Drew L. Hinds, Jr.
D.S.Y.A. Series managed by Vision Ink Corp.
Cover Photography by: Drew L. Hinds, Jr.
(www.drewlhinds.com)
visioninkauthor@yahoo.com

Written by: Drew L. Hinds, Jr.

Edited by: Lavatryce Griffin

Vision Ink Publishing
P.O. Box 10547
Riviera Beach, FL
33419

I0099163

Printed in United States of America

ISBN-10: 0983521433
ISBN-13: 978-0-9835214-3-3

Library of Congress Control Number: 2012947088

DREW L HINDS

POETIC SOUL
(The Simple Joys of Life)

A Book of Poems
VOLUME: 1

2012

"Without true, unconditional love there can be no genuine success, only petty vanity and deceit." – **DREW L. HINDS 2012**

Dedicated to all my loyal readers who love poetry

&

Sickle Cell Awareness

SICKLE CELL ANEMIA

In this book, I would like to bring awareness to the disease we know as Sickle Cell Anemia. This disease is prominent in people of African and Mediterranean descent, yet not limited to. It is also a hereditary disease caused by abnormal type of hemoglobin S. Hemoglobin (protein) carries oxygen within the blood cell, but become shaped like sickles and delivers less oxygen to the body's tissue. Some inherit the Sickle Cell Trait and do not suffer from the disease. These individuals must be mindful that if they have children with another person who has the trait, then the offspring most likely will inherit the disease.

Common symptoms:

- Yellowing of the eyes and skin (jaundice)

- Attacks of abdominal pain

- Paleness

- Breathlessness

- Delayed growth and puberty

- Fatigue

- Fever

- Bone pain

- Rapid heart rate

- Ulcers on the lower legs

Other symptoms:

- Painful and prolonged erection

- Skin ulcers

- Chest pain
- Poor eyesight/blindness
- Frequent urination
- Excessive thirst
- Strokes

DREW L. HINDS, AUTHOR OF:

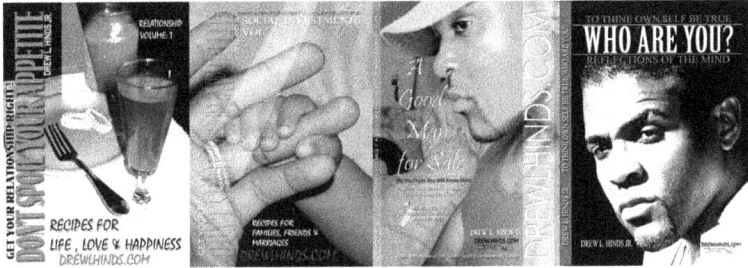

WHO ARE YOU?

A GOOD MAN FOR SALE

DON'T SPOIL YOUR APPETITE (DSYA) SERIES:
VOLUME: 1 **RELATIONSHIP**: RECIPES FOR LIFE, LOVE, &
HAPPINESS
VOLUME: 2 **SOCIAL INVESTMENTS**: RECIPES FOR
FAMLIES, FRIENDS & MARRIAGE

"DON'T SPOIL YOUR APPETITE" is a surprising delightful read.
This is not just another 'RELATIONSHIP" book, it is so much more.
This author has mastered the craft of telling a story that grabs you
from start to finish with his unique style of storytelling, poetry and
some good recipes to top it off. The book explores relationships in
a way that everyone can identify with. It transcends gender, genre,
generations, time, and ethnicity. It really gets to what's important to
you, in you, and for you, to be successful in any relationship.

The situations and characters may be fictional, but they were so
vibrant and realistic that I was able to identify and embrace them with
a sense of familiarity and truth. Truly a realistic, informative read with
the right touch of wit, humor and spirituality for you to keep reading
and wanting more. I intend to purchase this book for all my male,

female, single and married friends. Unequivocally, one of the best books I have had the pleasure of reading in a long time. Well done Mr. Hinds. Now that I have had a taste, I am hungry for your next book and I definitely will not spoil my appetite." – Annette Williams 2011 (Book Review)

CONTENTS

LOVE

LIFE

SPIRTUALITY

FINAL WORDS

AUTHOR'S CORNER

"For a good man naturally works for what is good and does so for his own sake, that is, for the sake of the intellectual part of his nature, which seems to be in every man his true self."
- ARISTOTLE, Nicomachean Ethics

Drew L. Hinds served in the Army Florida National Guard for six years, and acquired an Army Achievement Medal prior to ending his tour of serves. He attended Palm Beach Community State College and pursued his Criminal Justice Undergraduate studies, and is a certified law enforcement officer. Today he enjoys his time as a father, husband, mentor, author, photographer, graphic designer, lecturer, and as an operational director for Vision Ink Publishing. Drew Hinds has written and published his, "Don't Spoil Your Appetite/ Self Help Series." He has appeared at numerous events as guest speaker: the 2009 Harlem Book Fair in New York, the 2008 Raise the Praise Youth Convention in Toronto, On, Canada, the Riviera Beach Library Author's Night in 2010, and has been interviewed by numerous radio programs. As a Police Officer, he has interviewed hundreds of Domestic Violence victims and their families. He also has been featured in the compilation book, Dreams of Enchantment (The International Library of Poetry), as a member of The International Library of Poetry, and they have given him numerous awards.

Author Drew L. Hinds, Jr. writes in hopes of improving the quality of life for all through character building & spiritual awareness. Mr. Hinds was featured in the Palm Beach Post on January 5, 2012, in the Neighborhood Post, page 4, by the title, "Riviera cop writes self-help books as therapy for violence he witnesses." He also has been interviewed by '93 Emmy Award-Winning, News Anchor Juan Carlos Fanjul, CBS Channel 12 News, which was aired and entitled,

"Self-help author 'on duty'." This young talented author needs no introduction in Palm Beach County, FL and hopes to bring more awareness to the battle against Domestic Violence, Cancer and Sickle Cell Anemia globally.

This is a 2008 interview of Drew L. Hinds by Sheree M. Denton, prior to the release of this book:

Drew L. Hinds, Jr., a driven young man whose inner being radiates passion and a deep level of insight. Within the expanse of his geographical area, he has been described as compassionate and sincere, jovial yet professional, intelligent yet modest; all being a few of the qualities that make him admirable. Drew has the aptitude to operate in the capacity of a mentor, songwriter, vocalist, freelance photographer, self-taught pianist, and author (Debut book being *Don't Spoil Your Appetite, Volume 1*). In the form of vocation, Drew has served his country in the Military for eight years, where he acquired an Army Achievement Medal. Currently, he works as a Police Officer, in Florida, where he received a Bureau Commendation for going "above and beyond" the call of duty.

Born to the proud parents Mr. and Mrs. Andrew L. Hinds Sr., Drew made his entry into this world in Brooklyn, New York, in the year of 1977. Unfortunately, due to the premature death of his father, Drew was deprived of those precious father-son moments, at a very early age in life. This loss proved to be the foundational element of a pivotal moment in his life, in which he culminated his relationship with the Lord; realizing that he needs Him to be his *Earthly* Father as well as his *Heavenly* Father. Drew expresses his memory of God being his "imaginary friend or daddy" at the age of two, therefore making *God* his *daddy*, how awesome. The protection and consolation he receives from his "God Daddy," has given him the desire to be there for some other child. In fact, Drew is affectionately called by many children "God Daddy Drew;" as he has bridged the gap, by allowing himself to be God's instrumental tool of encouragement and pure untainted love for these children. Taking up this responsibility, not having any children of his own until his recent marriage, one can say this young man surely posses the quintessence of selflessness.

 "Live the dream, write the vision," is the motto that Drew lives by, and the disciplined method in which he deals with his goals. His deepest endeavor is to enlighten those who have lost hope, as he himself has been a victim of the same; recovered by the help of God and through self-motivation. - Sheree M. Denton 2008

ACKNOWLEDGEMENTS

"As everyone follows traditions of men, be liberated & study the origin. Knowledge is power, & I love the power you can possess." – DREW L. HINDS JR. 2011

I am very excited that I have been so moved to write a book of poems, and it is only by the grace of God that I am inspired to write. I would like to take the time to express my appreciation to everyone who has helped from behind the scenes, sharing their talents and inspirations with me throughout this journey.

"To thine own self be true." Being a liar is bad, but lying to yourself is just pitiful. Wake up!" – **DREW L. HINDS 2011**

To all my young people and godchildren, thank you for keeping me smiling, I pray that you will be blessed and highly favored in the Lord. To all my immediate family, friends, supporters and readers, I love you, and may God bless you all. My heart goes out to those who are overwhelmed by the stress of life. *Lord, I know we have nothing worthy enough to offer in exchange, but we give ourselves. I pray that if there is anything amongst us that will hinder this prayer that you will remove it from our countenance, in Jesus name...Amen!"*

I do hope and pray that I have continued to inspire and captivate an awareness of spirituality and a continuous respect for life, as we know it. I have prayed my prayer once again over this book:

"Behold, who am I that I have found favor in my Father's eye? So much so that he has bestowed His blessings on one such as me. I have not earned my wealth, yet I receive it bountifully. Lead me to a place of understanding, so that I may fathom thy will of me, oh' Father.

I live to serve you all the days of my life. You have acknowledged my wants and have provided my needs. You have heard my silent prayers and blessed me openly. I stand before you as a new creation and I live on with a new hope."

"God has more in store for your life than you could ever imagine, just be still and know that He has your future all planned out."

– DREW L. HINDS 2011

INTRODUCTION

"To thine own self be true"- Shakespeare
(*Hamlet Act 1, scene 3*).

This book of poems was created to accommodate the overwhelming positive response to my poetry. So, with that said, I collected many of my poems from my previous books and compiled them into one book, "Just to wet the appetite," as I would say. I have always tried to give words of encouragement. This book of poems was meant to awaken my readers to the poetic soul in all of us. Please be mindful that we as a people are battling against Domestic Violence, Breast Cancer and various other causes globally, so continue to show your support.

TRIALS

I have come to a realization that for one to know what they are truly made of they must go through some rough times as a test of their inner strength. I know many of us face different challenges in our lives and we get discouraged at times. We fail to understand that once we endure through our trials, we only become stronger in character. You know the old, "No Pain, No Gain," slogan. I want you to know that you are not alone, and there are people who truly care about you. One way to find out who cares about you is first become a good friend yourself. Like they say, "It takes one to know one." If we adopt the mind set, "That the race is not for the swift, but for the one that endures till the end," (KJV) then and only then can we persevere through the race of life.

APPRECIATE

Do me a favor, and let someone close too you know how much you appreciate him or her. The reason I say this is because we seem to always wait till something bad happens to share our true feelings towards each other. Furthermore, you never know who in your life may need to hear that encouraging word. "So spread some love and watch it come back to you."

A PURPOSE

"There will always be the selfish yearning, but the trick is not to yield to your desires."
  – DREW L. HINDS 2012

        I have found that I have been in a state of doubt, concerning myself. I believe that it is due to the fact that I have never really understood what God had in store for my life. It also has a lot to do with me not understanding that God would use me for His will. I say this for a few simple reasons. First, there are many of us who are under a false pretense that God only uses educated scholars, righteous church members, financially stable citizens, in essence, "perfect people," to do His work. In all honesty, that is not the case. God doesn't use perfect people, but willing people." In fact no matter what your stature is in life, you can only be used if you are truly willing to be used.

I started a "Text Message Ministry," which consisted of me sending memory verses daily. I never realized the impact that it had until I forgot to send a text one day and to my surprise, I received numerous text and phone calls reprimanding me for not sending a text out. There were some who said that they relied on my "Daily Devotional Text" as a mini devotional to start their day. Some stated that they forward the texts to friends and family for inspiration. I really never knew that God could use something as simple as a text to inspire others. So, in closing, please "Don't try to be perfect in your Christian walk, just be willing," because I wouldn't want you too spoil your appetite or your poetic soul…. (smile).

LOVE

"Wisdom is the act of knowing when to utilize the knowledge you have obtained." - DREW L. HINDS 2006

WHO AM I TO SPEAK?

Who am I to speak on the topic of love you ask

I am just a simple man who has been in love once or twice

But have been loved by many I still don't know

I have been told that I have enlightened those who would listen

But yet I find that I am still learning

I have experienced love, the emotion

Yet I have taught others the principle of love

I have been tricked by love on occasion

but I have charismatically persuaded my share

I have been humbled by love

But I have found strength in it as well

I have been known to be conditional with love

But God is teaching me Ag-ape love daily

Love is the essence of who I am

But then again who am I to speak about love

"My biggest fear is being emotionally numb, a state where I cannot give or receive love." - DREW L. HINDS 2008

FROM A DISTANCE

It's funny, I am alone and love her from a distance in silence

She knew she always had my heart and I was fulfilled

I was lost when love found rescue in my best friend's embrace

Yet in the midst of pain, I confess I still loved her continuously

Love lost the child she bore for him

and then had another for someone else

She begged for my forgiveness

and I left physically but never emotionally

It's funny I am alone and love her from a distance in silence

To be honest I have always been in love with love

and she with me

I left love behind each time she hurt me

Yet every time I still loved

I have been fooled by love

Yet I still embrace her essence, her voice

I can remember love

In her different shades, shapes, and heights

I can remember love with her many accents, faces and moods

It's funny I am alone and love her from a distance in silence

I awake from countless dreams of her embrace

and yet stay alone

I fear love, for she has deceived me

Yet I love the life she breaths into me

I run from love

because I remember how vulnerable she has made me

Yet I long for love

When the night is still and the air is calm serene

I still hear love wooing me in my dreams

In her usual alluring way

It's funny I am alone and love her from a distance in silence

"A man that chooses a woman with his whole heart, has made a
decision for life and is not scared to tell all."

– DREW L.HINDS 2012

IF YOU KNEW

I thank the Lord that I found you

God could only know

You're a part of me, I want all to see

Love inconceivable

Take me to have and to hold

Forever and a day, and I promise you

That I do, love you for always

"Just imagine how it would feel to be a motivating factor in someone's life that they would hang on your every word. It's priceless, just to say the least." – DREW L. HINDS 2012

YOU ARE

You are poetry in motion

Stimulating my deepest thoughts

Heightening my awareness of life

Provoking my heart to learn

You are one extended song

Melodiously filling my thoughts

Arousing the thought of love

Soothing my weary spirit

You are spoken words

With a hint of spirituality

Accented with a touch of self-motivation

Illuminating a doubtful heart

You are what you are

Mine now and forever more

"To my surprise, she noticed me and gently took my hand. Then I
knew that I would be blessed to be her man."

- DREW L. HINDS (Song Lyrics) Could it be chance 2003

TO MY SIGNIFICANT OTHER

I heed to your call, my love

I too yearn for the warm embrace of your femininity

Endless days of bliss, forever nights of pleasure

Our love entrusted since the beginning of creation

Lingering on 'til the end of life probation

I must know my love 'twas it my heart you sought

Or was it just lustfulness for my anatomy

Tell me it is not so, 'cause I would hate to let you go

But as we both know, life will go on as it has and as it will

I'm not willing to submit my physical essence to you

Without sincerity and ownership of your mind

"Love can illuminate the darkest heart, so when you decide to love,
just love as hard as you can." – DREW L. HINDS 2012

ILLUMINATING MY LIFE

To my caramel ray of sunshine

You are my moon, illuminating my life

With your words of wisdom

You are my air, filling my lungs

A positive vibe of subtle reassurance

You are my mentor

Holding my heart in the balance of your smile

You move me, in ways not known

To a bachelor's consciousness

You have won my admiration, many times over

You inspire me to create and recreate my inner being

Dissolving my stubborn awkwardness

You complete my thoughts, my hypothesis of life

Of love and happiness

Last, but not least, you complete me

Illuminating my life with your words of wisdom

"Honesty can cleanse the darkest soul and rejuvenate one's inner
spirit, but sincerity in ones remorse signifies true hope for change."
 - DREW L. HINDS 2008

SHE IS MY FAMILY

I dare not remember a time without you

I dare not sing a song without you in mind

I dare not write without you in view

I dare not imagine you shedding a tear on my behalf

I dare not fathom you not a part of me, my family

I dare not dream of how my life would be without you

I dare not allow myself to feel grief for claiming you first

I dare not share your love with anyone alive or passed

I dare not run from you my love, or what we have

I dare not excuse my ignorance of how you have changed me

I dare not think of losing you

I dare not

"If you ever have a chance to love, take and run with it. Some only get one chance, so embrace it like it is your last."

- DREW L. HINDS 2012

LOVE GAVE ME A CHOICE

No one wants to be alone

Well, no one I know

No one runs from love

Well, no one that is brave enough to fight for it

No one gives their heart and forgets who has it

Well, no one in their right mind wants to forget

No one cries like me or writes like me

Well, no one who fought for love and exhausted their fight

No one can imagine love (eros) germinates into a tangible being

Well, no one can imagine I met her and let her go

No one knows why I am writing these words

Well, no one that hasn't felt the same way

No one loves someone they can't have

Well, no one knows me well

No one

"My heart has always led me to a place I call home, and so I am renewed in my time of need." - DREW L. HINDS 2008

I REMEMBERED YOU MOM

Oh mommy, I am glad you came to my rescue

I can always call on you in my issue

You cater to me and all I go through

You're supportive and loving

And stand by with tissue

I pray you won't change for years to come

I want to say thanks, but there's a lump sum to say

On my heart on my mind, I could never repay

I just want you to know I love and miss you

Forever your child

"It does hurt to find an open means of communication with Love. In fact, it saves us from assumptions and unnecessary pain."

– DREW L. HINDS 2012

SILENT THOUGHTS SPEAK

Some know her and call her Love

I was introduced before, yet I fear her

She moves me without my permission

I consciously restrain my will, yet she compels me

I pray she never resorts to deliberately pursuing my longing lips

She has discovered my hidden void and has exposed me

I hid from her watchful eye, yet she sees my detached emotion

Symbolically, she is aware of her place, her destiny, my rib

Yet, still I await in silence, overwhelmed with emotion and lust

Only God knows my desire or my conviction

Often tears comfort me

No words or imagery can express the longing I possess

No kind word can ease this emptiness of loneliness

It is not good for man to be alone and I believe it now

Where forth art thee my helpmate, my spouse

We are all creations, created with a purpose

To give and receive love is that purpose

Yet still I wait alone and silent

Still I wait with hope

Still I hope

Still just I

Just…I

I alone

"For one to realize who they are and act on the realization, in hopes of bringing about a

positive self-purifying result, is truly awesome. When loved ones are there to witness the inception of your germination, the transition is made easier." - DREW L. HINDS 2008

MENTAL INTIMACY

Why is it that you can speak to my spirit?

Who gave you authority over my admiration?

Why is it that I can't escape your longing gaze?

Why do you have me lingering on your every word?

Why do I confess my most intimate thoughts to you?

Why does your opinion hold so much value in my eyes?

Why have I waited so long to be moved by a remarkable you?

Why is it that you make me question why you are intimate

With my mind?

"Love is kind, it forgives and allows us to partake of its virtue in spite of our imperfections." - DREW L. HINDS 2012

IN SPITE OF MYSELF

Love, I give you credit…yes, I really do

You love (Eros) me in spite of what I say and do

Lord knows, it's not easy to love me in spite of myself

I am militant and stern, but you love me in spite of myself

I have little or no patience, but you love me in spite of myself

I am often consumed by my thoughts

but you love me in spite of myself

I only respond to a response, but you love me in spite of myself

God knows me and you, but still you love me in spite of myself

I pray God continues to give you patience

To endure me and my ways

I pray that God will alter my harsh and militant ways

I pray for your spiritual growth as I test you on days

In spite of myself, please know I love you always

"A remarkable yet mutual self disclosure was achieved by both of us, and we became a reflection of our love."

- DREW L. HINDS 2008

I AM ENGAGED TO LOVE

God has a sense of humor

Rightly I say so over and over to myself

I have watched, I have prayed and I have waited for His answer

Somehow by myself, of myself

I could not find a resolve to my void

This has not been the first time that love had left me

Weary, alone and silent

I have loved and lost

and it had become a familiar cliché that was unwelcome

Finally I stopped trying,

Stopped looking

and stopped praying for a change in my relations

I had decided that love had left a familiar bad taste

for the last time

I had removed my mind from ever fathoming my own helpmate

I had turned a deaf ear to peers questioning if I was happy

I had overlooked the fact

that only God can introduce me to my future

Funny though

how my future had become my present confidante and friend

Funny though

how my friend had easily become my present love

Without touching me

For the first time I had fallen in love with love's characteristics

Overlooking her smile

For the first time I had released my fear of love

Embracing her wisdom and her honesty

Finally my guards were let down

And love saw that I had closed the door not locking it

My fears of letting love in to see my vulnerability subsided,

A willing student

Love had consulted with God prior to finding me

And knew my previous prayers

God has a sense of humor,

He knew I would finally surrender my being to true love

I no longer fear love, yet I embrace what it is and will be,

mine now and forever more

So to God and man I do declare this day

That I am engaged with love

And she with me

"It is a humbling experience to grasp, that a person of no relation can appreciate your true inner worth and give without regard for a return."

 - DREW L. HINDS 2008

A PRAYER ANSWERED

I have always dreamed of having a lady in my life,

a friend, confidant, a mate dare I say, wife

Funny though, I almost lost hope,

and here you are, a prayer answered

I always dreamed of conversing with a woman

who knows my heart,

who is one with my spirit, and feels my joy when I smile

Funny though, I almost lost hope,

and here you are, a prayer answered

Many nights I pondered of sharing a ministry

with my significant other,

and thanking God for blessing me with my own spiritual being.

Funny though, I almost lost hope,

and here you are, a prayer answered.

I stopped dreaming and praying for a better half

for quite some time now,

and went on living unfulfilled.

Funny though, I almost lost hope,

and here you are, a prayer answered.

I thank God for you, every day of my life,

and know that God had interceded on my behalf.

Funny though, I almost lost hope,

and here you are, a prayer answered.

"A marriage doesn't define a person, but in essence a defined person should partake in the symbolic testament called marriage."
- DREW L. HINDS 2008

I HAVE LEARNED

I have learned to give and receive love

I have learned love takes time and patience

I have learned love is an unconscious investment

I have learned my heart can sometimes lead me astray

I have learned the difference between love and lust

I have learned that all that glitters is not love

I have learned that I can be moved by mental intimacy

I have learned to love a woman inside out

I have learned to listen more and talk less

I have learned to allow love to humble me

I have learned that all need love, yet some may resist

I have learned some have mental baggage and fear love

I have learned that I am inspired by love in its true essence

I have learned that I am moved by love the verb

I have learned that I have the ability to persuade

and awaken love

I have learned that love doesn't always know what's best for me

I have learned that I have loved the notion

of my vulnerability to love

I have learned that someday

I will have to stop running from love

I have learned that someday the right love (Eros) will catch me

I have learned that now I am not scared to let love catch me

I have learned, yes believe it or not, I have learned

"It is simply captivating when one acknowledges the realization that the mere essence and existence of their relationship is truly unique and absolute. To finally comprehend that no other being can replicate either party's contribution, in itself brings utter fulfillment."

 - DREW L. HINDS 2008

I'VE GROWN

I've grown to appreciate your smile, as warm as a sunset

I've grown accustomed to your words of encouragement

Like no other I've met

I've grown close to your wisdom, and heartfelt nightly prayers

I've grown needy for your voice, I no longer idolize players

I've grown out of the realization of give and take

Yet it's give and give

I've grown past my selfish motive

and you have given me reason to live

I've grown into the idea of you being around indefinitely

I've grown to finally understand

that you complete me completely

"If we encourage in love, then we can inspire others to live up to their true potential, and in essence let go of acquired self doubt."

 - DREW L. HINDS 2008

IF ONLY I KNEW

To be honest

I never knew how much you brought to my life

To be revealed and exposed

I never loved anyone like you

To be moved by verbal expression

She whispered to me, ever so softly

I am not an option, yet a privilege

To be honest, if only I knew

"Knowing someone from the inside out goes deeper than a superficial observation; yet it is a true mental intimacy that transcends time and space." – DREW L. HINDS 2009

DID YOU KNOW?

I have leaned on you for support

With a heart of youth

I feel safe in thinking that

I can rely on your un-bias truth

I thank God for you

And the realizations you bring to my life

So, forgive me if I have always

Considered you as my wife

"She saw my true potential, and encouraged me to excel. I was never confined by her, yet defined and my heart was renewed by her smile."
 - DREW L. HINDS 2008

IN VISION ME

A forbidden touch of love

Can render a willing lonely heart helpless

A comforting and lingering embrace

Can reassure a doubtful and longing spirit

A seductive yet gentle enduring kiss

Can utterly immobilize those faint at heart

A sincere compliment from an honest soul

Can rejuvenate a bewildered and broken spirit

A stimulating and intellectual conversation

Can arouse an uncharted mental intimacy

A man with a vision and willingness to learn

Can win his woman's heart over with a smile

"Isn't it wonderful to be chosen by Love? I can say from personal experience that it is wonderful to give and receive Love in its purest form." – DREW L. HINDS 2012

JUST REMARKABLE

I pondered the notion, what you see is what you get

Why you ask, because I can't believe you picked me

I am much more than a chiseled frame, meet my sound mind

I have often pondered how one can judge a book by its cover

I have found that words can reveal the heart of a man

A man is more than what is seen, if you look closer

Many of us hide behind our rough exterior in self-defense

We rely on the notion that we are the strong silent type

There are many of us who long to share a thought

There are many who seek mental intimacy

There are many who yearn for love, in its purest form

There are many of us who wish you could see the real man

There are many of us who are weary of searching

for a remarkable you

In reality there are only a few

that may have the chance to meet you

Now isn't that just remarkable?

"One should reveal their true expectations in the conception of a
union to avoid misconceptions and future strife."

- DREW L. HINDS 2009

JUST FOR ME

I choose you for you, I love your eyes

I choose you to calm my spirit, I love your shapely curves

I choose you to inspire my vision, I love your warm embrace

I choose you to bring me back to reality, I love your soft kiss

I choose you to love me in and out of season

I love your honesty

I choose you to bare my child, I love your mental intimacy

I choose you to pray for me, I love your seductive gaze

I choose you for so many reasons, but mostly it was just for me

"A relationship shouldn't be merely an obligation dictated by a condition, if for any reason this occurs it becomes equivalent to a job." – DREW L. HINDS 2009

JUST LISTEN

Trust me, there is a lot you don't know

Trust me, there is a lot I want to tell

At times I am not sure you want to know

Then again I could be wrong

I am scared to be vulnerable

I think you're scared as well

Yes, I don't think the way you do

But that is what makes it interesting

Your moodiness intrigues me

I watch your smile as well as your hips

I love your smell, your touch

I close my eyes and I remember your taste

You seem to know my needs

I love that you're eager to learn me

We have something in common

I love your femininity, it is alluring to my eye

If you would just be still

I have more to share, just listen

"Women need emotional security, but men need a tangible source of physical connection to achieve the equivalent of her emotion."

– DREW L. HINDS 2009

I'M YOUR MAN

Yes, I am with you for more reasons than one

Trust me, it's not for your finances, you're broke

I love when you don't question me

Then again, I planned on telling you anyway

You're beautiful, even though you lost your shape

I know you gained since we first met, so what

I like that you know me and can make me smile

You seem to know when to stop me before I lose it

Then again you know how to get me started

I can't stand you at times, but I am helpless alone

So, yes I am your man, what else is new

"Recognition expresses appreciation which is equivalent to a sense of belonging." – DREW L. HINDS 2009

MY REWARD

I still can't believe that you are mine

You give me such joy as you beckon my intimacy

Your lips stay sweet, as if to summon my masculinity

I long for your kiss, which is light yet fulfilling

You have given life to a hopeless man

I yearn for your seductive embrace

Your body caters to my longing

I am at ease in your bosom

I forget my woes inside your love

I am blessed to have you

My love

My friend

My reward

"Men think black and white simply because they are rational creatures, so they will express their discomfort. The trick is to listen and empathize, regardless of your own perspective."
– DREW L. HINDS 2009

RELAX

I am with you by choice, not by court order, so relax

I paid the parking meter as well as your mom's bill, so relax

I love you regardless of your new size, so relax

I am sorry you had a rough day at work, but it's Friday, so relax

I am sorry the recipe came out wrong, we can eat out, so relax

I know you can only work part time as a student

that's why I work, so relax

You can't have any more kids, well neither can I afford it

So relax

No really, relax

"Why initiate a relationship on false pretense? In essence, it has no substance or longevity." – DREW L. HINDS 2009

QUESTION

Please be honest with me, I am curious

Where do you go after we argue?

Is that really your hair, if not, how much was it?

Do you really think your mom hates me?

Why does your male boss always call you after hours?

Have you dated some of your male friends?

Is it me, or do you hate when I go to the gym alone?

Why do you always ask for money when you get paid?

If you're my woman, why do you always seem too busy for me?

Why do you always leave the gas tank empty?

When it's your time of the month, can I work late?

To be honest, I am happy, I was just curious

LIFE

"Life has a way of defining who we are and what we stand for, so reflect daily on your purpose and goals." – DREW L. HINDS 2012

ME

I think, therefore I am what I know and feel

The essence of what I believe

Surrounded by a misguided environment

Still inspired by the innocence of youth

Yet, still molded by elderly wisdom

"Sometimes you have to let go of what you want, so God can give you what you need." - DREW L. HINDS 2007

I CALL HER FRIEND

I call her friend, yet none other moves me with their sigh

Her concern for my well being, astonishes me

and her voice soothes my restless mind

I call her friend, though I wonder what if, and what could be

She understands when none other listens

She cares when none other calls

She worries when no one else knows my woes

I call her friend, but she means much more to me

She is the essence of my life that makes life worth living

Caring, loving, but, I just call her friend, and my friend is music

"A single mother can raise a nation and deserves riches untold, but yet settles for a thank you mommy." – DREW L. HINDS 2012

A SINGLE MOTHER SMILES AT ME

A single mother smiles at me

She admires my voice, my gentle eyes

I long for her words of inspiration

I hear her heart through her words

She is trapped in her emotions

She finds freedom in sharing her past

She has loved in life and remembers joy

She embraces a dream that no one else knows

She cries when no one else sees

Her soul cries for freedom

But her existence goes on unnoticed

Still a single mother smiles at me

"We all have learned beliefs and standards of living that shape our character. One shouldn't give up who they are to justify their allegiance to a significant other, they will lose self worth."

– DREW L. HINDS 2009

SIMPLY A PRIVILEGE

You are my God, by conviction not confusion

You are my friend, by choice not by chance

You are my mentor, by inspiration not eloquence

You are my love, by value not intimacy

You are my family, by your untiring dedication not lineage

You are my employer, by decision not desperation

You are my associate, by tolerance not status

It is true, life will go on as it has and as it will

You are what you are, a privilege to me, not a right

"It is essential for one to self examine themselves and correct their flaws before it destroys them." – DREW L. HINDS 2012

MY REFLECTION

I am a leader with no title

A teacher with no students

I have chosen a mission, one that has no visible reward

I support those who have no voice

My work is visible

My intent is known

My joy is shared with those who have grown

Under my watchful eye

I pray all succeed

I pray all will grow

I pray the Spirit of God will touch those He knows

"Life, in general, can be so cruel," are the words that ran through my mind as a child explained to me her horrific encounter with her uncle. I hung my head at times when it became too unbearable to imagine. For unknown reasons, my utility belt I was wearing felt constricting around my waist. My hands stayed close to my face covering my mouth. My eyes stayed fixed on the young child as she trembled in fear as I adjusted my badge on my freshly pressed uniform and reluctantly listened and envisioned her fear. I still hear her voice haunting me as she shared her story…(Sigh)."

HER INNOCENCE SPEAKS

I am scared, so scared

Yet I dare not scream

I dare not speak, I dare not move

I feel helpless yet no one comes to my aid

This is not the first time, but I pray it is the last

Oh God, deliver me I have no will to live through this

I am only a child, I am only a scared child imprisoned in my fear

There is no safe place for me, no one sees or hears my cries

I was innocent once, but he touched me too many times

I don't feel like a child anymore, I don't feel human

I don't feel anymore, I just exist, I just survive

He has stripped me of more than my clothing

I am always scared, I fear even fear itself

My paranoia has consumed my very being

I am alone, no one else knows, no one sees

Oh, no he is coming for me again

I can't scream, I fear him too much

I can't cry, he feeds on my terror

I can't hope anymore

I can't remember my innocence

"We all need to know that there is someone that we can find that refuge. I have chosen to find it in a higher being that control space and time, because He alone is my potter and I, His clay."

– DREW L. HINDS 2012

MY REFUGE

I have found refuge under your watchful eye

And your motives have been revealed over time

I have also learned my true identity in your presence

And thus have come to appreciate your essence

We have grown together through obvious trials

Yet persevered the endless unforgiving miles

These irreplaceable times will always provide vivid memories

So after it is all said and done

We are still what we know as, my family

Indeed my friend when I am in need

"The principles that one lives by will in turn be the same that sustains him till death." - DREW L. HINDS 2009

STAND

Stand when no one else understands your purpose

Stand when family and friends turn their backs on you

Stand, because you are being true to yourself

Stand after you have fallen time and time again

Stand when no one else supports your cause

Stand for something or fall for anything

Stand, because it is what Jesus would do

Stand in the midst of adversity and fear

Stand when no one else will

Stand, because…you can

You can stand!

"A relationship truly is a selfless component of life that one must be

mature in character to initiate and patient enough to maintain."

 – DREW L. HINDS 2009

I NEED YOU

I have a lot on my mind, would you listen?

I had a rough day, can you hold me?

I almost lost it today, can you relate?

I have lost hope, would you pray?

I received some bad news, would you stay?

It really isn't getting any easier, can you love me?

I'm glad I am not alone, it's times like this when I need you

Please, know that I need you

"Relationship is not a power struggle, yet a union of mind body and spirit." – DREW L. HINDS 2009

I WONDER

I wonder what she is thinking when I am late

I wonder what she is thinking when I make excuses

I wonder why she tolerates my impatient nature

I wonder if she noticed I broke her curling iron

I wonder what her and her friends talk about

I wonder if I was just another one of her options

I wonder why she gets quiet when I leave the toilet seat up

I wonder why she never tells me her pain

Sometimes, I wonder how long it will last

Yes, I wonder

SPIRITUALITY

"We all need mentoring, whether in our personal, professional or
spiritual growth." – DREW L. HINDS 2012

COACHING A MAN'S SPIRIT

I have admired your growth, don't lose focus

Your whole temperament has changed, stay humble

You have overcome great obstacles, but you have many to face

Allow yourself to live a sincere existence, don't stray from truth

Embrace your innocence, disregard your vanity

Cultivate your childlike forgiveness

disregard your mental baggage

Continue to find the simple joys of life

overlook other's mistakes

Help those who need your wisdom, avoid those that corrupt you

Find peace of mind in honesty, rebuke the spirit of deceit

Pray for a reformation of character, let go of selfishness

Embrace a revival of spirit, be aware of negative people

Always pray for a renewed mind, body, and soul

For it will be the key to life, love and spirituality

"We all have been overwhelmed by life, but the true strength of a man's character is his ability to endure."

– DREW L. HINDS 2012

DAMAGED NOT DESTROYED

I have been through it all, yet I am still standing

I have been overwhelmed in this life

by issues so demanding

I am grateful to those who have inspired me to carry on

I am thankful that God has always strengthened me

with a song

I hope and pray that I will endure through many more trials

Whether great or small

give me the faith to overcome them all

I am more than a conquer

and I have lived through many of sleepless nights

I have forgotten more trials then I care to remember

and I am still here

Yes, I am still here to tell the story of how I got over

Yes, I am still alive to be grateful that I endured

Yes, I am still a living reminder that you can make it

Yes, I am damaged, but I am not destroyed

To God be the glory, great things He has done

"When a man can believe enough to risk it all on something that only their heart can validate, then he is indeed a man of faith."

– DREW L. HINDS 2012

WALKING BY FAITH

Many times I have no clue how it will all work out

Many times I have no choice but hope for the best

Many times I have prayed for solutions

Many times I have had to be patient and have faith

Many times I have found my relief

Faith has helped me through many times

"If you can dream it, you can achieve it by faith."

– DREW L. HINDS 2012

DREAMING THE IMPOSSIBLE

I can do all things by faith

I can make my dreams a reality

The impossible is possible if I believe

With this in mind I am often relieved

I can achieve my goals

I can overcome my foes

The key is to never stop believing

Never stop dreaming things worth achieving

"Forgiveness is not solely for the offender, yet more so the victim.
One most forgive first to begin the healing process."

 – DREW L. HINDS 2012

FORGIVEN

Time after time I have made mistakes

Time after time I have apologized

Remarkably every time I have been forgiven

I made choices that I can't take back

I made plans that were selfish

Remarkably every time I have been forgiven

I understand now that forgiveness leads to healing

I understand now that healing equates to spiritual balance

Still it's remarkable every time I have been forgiven

" I am a creation, therefore I was created. If I was created, therefore I
have a Creator. If I have a creator, then I was created with a purpose."
– DREW L. HINDS 2012

WHAT IS MY PURPOSE

I know the unspoken truth

I am wonderfully and fearfully made

I am a creation with a creator

I was created to serve my creator

I am my potter's clay

I will serve my maker

I exist solely to live out my purpose

My purpose is to help other creations

"My God has never failed me, and I find strength in knowing that he will provide." – DREW L. HINDS 2012

FINDING MY STRENGTH

The road of life has never been easy

Then again nothing worth having has ever been easy

All and all I have found inner strength

All and all I have found a spiritual balance

All and all I have found peace

I have lived for others and have been blessed

I have been admired for my calmness

Yet I find strength in composure

I find strength in knowing that I am never alone

My faith is my strength and my refuge

"I haven't always been strong, but I have made it this far by faith."

– DREW L. HINDS 2012

I HAVE COME THIS FAR

I remember those of old clear as day

I have come this far by faith

I could not agree more

I remember my mother clear as day

If you don't hear you will feel

I could not agree more

I remember what I have learned clear as day

If you don't stand for something you'll fall for anything

I could not agree more

I remember this thought clear as day

I have come too far to turn back now

Remembering my past, I could not agree more

"I have overcome many obstacles in my life to get where I am, and I refuse to look back." – DREW L. HINDS 2012

NO LOOKING BACK

Why look back, I live with no regrets?

Why play "The what if game," when my steps were all ordained?

Why should I remember bad habits I have conquered?

Why revisit old temptations I have overcome?

Why doubt the decisions I have made yesterday?

Why ponder on past fears I have surpassed?

Why question what I have gained and lack?

I am serious, why look back?

"I know I'm not perfect and I have made many mistakes, but if there is one thing I know I got right, and that is choosing God."

– DREW L. HINDS 2012

SELF-EXAMINTATION

I have prayed for a renewed mind

Still I am working on controlling my thoughts

I have studied many wise men

Still I crave for more knowledge

I have been scolded by my superiors

Still I require correction

I have corrected personal flaws

Still I need self-examination

"Many think they can play both fields, both good and evil; but in reality we can only choose one." – DREW L. HINDS 2012

LUKEWARM

As I see it, you are either hot or cold

Right or Wrong

As I see it, you are either good or evil

Light or Dark

As I see it, society has clouded our perceptions

We have become desensitized and immoral

As I see it, the world craves power and vanity

Yet we wonder why there is so much suffering

As I see it, adolescents of this time are misguided

Then again so are the adults

As I see it, we as a people need to regain morality

This will only happen when people return to knowing God

Well, as far I see it

"It's funny, I was taught to pray at meals, when I awake and bed times; but now I pray constantly to maintain my sanity."

– DREW L. HINDS 2012

A PRAYER

If prayer changes things

Then no prayer no change

If no prayer goes unnoticed

Then all fervent prayers avails much

If a prayer is not defined by its length

Then it is defined by its sincerity

If someone else prays on my behalf

Then it is an intercessory prayer

If I continually talk to God in my mind

Then I am praying without ceasing

If I pray with my face to the ground pleading with God

Then I am prostrating before Him

So, really prayer changes things

Then no prayer no change

"I can always count on the spirit of God to comfort me with a song of hope." – DREW L. HINDS 2012

YOU ARE MY SONG

I love music

It has always been a part of me

It gives me hope and calms my spirit

As a child of God I have embraced the hymnal sound

When I reflect on all that God has brought me through

I have to sing

I have to let Jehovah, my Emmanuel know my joy

I live to praise him in work and song

God is the words to my song of life

His spirit is the melody I hum

For God alone is the reason I sing

"I have tried living my life my way, but now I realize that no one knows a creation like it's creator." – DREW L. HINDS 2012

COMING HOME

Lord I know that it is I that has left your side

For you have said that you will never leave me nor forsake me

I appreciate the fact that as a father

you always welcome me back home

Words could not express the joy and relief of being accepted

You have forgiven time and time again with your Agape Love

I will forever be indebted to you in return for your love

I hope and pray I will be who you want me to be

I am tired of making my own decisions and failing

I am overwhelmed with the burdens of life

I have failed to foresee my enemies' plots

I am coming home to you

For you are my refuge

With you I am always home

"I often ask for forgiveness before I make a decision contrary to my discerning spirit." – DREW L. HINDS 2012

CONFESSION

Yes, confession is good for the soul,

but it leaves you vulnerable

I have yet to understand

why I have fallen for the same thing twice

I don't always know the right decision, but I give orders

I have prayed for more patience

Yet I tolerate adolescent mistakes

All in all, in each confession there is a lesson

"It is wise to be aware of the negative things that have taken over our lives and find a way to cut loose from them."

– DREW L. HINDS 2012

STRONG HOLDS

Oh Lord, if you would reach out to the broken hearted
Also, those who are stressed
and believers who have lost all hope
I pray that you would take them and free them from the bondage of
their pain
Lord, I am not asking for deliverance
based on any of us being worthy
Solely, because you are merciful
Forgive us of our sins and transgressions.
My heart is heavy and your people are so broken
Restore them Father; give them strength to hope again
Help us all to pray again, to sing again
to believe again, to love again
Teach us all to forgive again, to confess again,
and to rebuke again
Restore us to stand up again, and to dream again
Oh Lord, I know we have nothing worthy enough
to offer in exchange

So we give of ourselves entirely
I pray that if there is anything amongst us
that will hinder this prayer
that you will remove it from our countenance
in Jesus name...Amen!"

"Set short term and long term goals, and don't let anything hinder you from achieving your goals." – DREW L. HINDS 2012

DISTRACTIONS

All desires of the heart can corrupt the spirit

All desires of the eye can corrupt the mind

All desires of the flesh can corrupt the body

All desires inevitably become distractions

Final Words

"If it's in your power to help someone, then we as people should never withhold that assistance." – DREW L. HINDS 2008

My motto is, "*Live the dream and write the vision.*" My vision is: " The paths that I have traveled and the ones ahead are long and arduous. However, the knowledge, expertise, and morals that I have and will acquire along the way are invaluable. One of the most important moral principles that I have acquired thus far is that we sometimes have to let go of what we want in order for God to give us what we need. "

"In general, the proof of a person's knowledge or ignorance is his ability to teach. Hence, we consider art more truly knowledge than experience, for artists can teach and others cannot." - ARISTOTLE, Metaphysics

I know my weaknesses, so I avoid anything that may become a distraction. I also believe that through opportunity & disappointment God allows us to learn valuable lessons about ourselves & life. One of my goals is to inspire and encourage up-and-coming artists. Many people have forgotten from whence they came; however, I beg to differ. I am eager and willing to assist aspiring artists in whatever way I can. I encourage all to share their knowledge and experience with the upcoming generation. Finally, I want you to enjoy the simple joys of life. Be positive, poetic, and courageous as you give and receive love.

www.ingramcontent.com/pod-product-compliance
Lightning Source LLC
Chambersburg PA
CBHW062022040426
42447CB00010B/2102